HATSHEPSUT

Leaders of the Ancient World

HATSHEPSUT

Margaux Baum and

Susanna Thomas

ROSEN PUBLISHING

New York

Published in 2017 by The Rosen Publishing Group, Inc.
29 East 21st Street, New York, NY 10010

First Edition

Library of Congress Cataloging-in-Publication Data

Names: Baum, Margaux, author. | Thomas, Susanna, 1966– author.
Title: Hatshepsut / Margaux Baum and Susanna Thomas.
Description: First edition. | New York, NY : The Rosen Publishing Group, Inc., 2017. | Series: Leaders of the ancient world | Includes bibliographical references and index. | Audience: Grades 7–12.
Identifiers: LCCN 2016030398 | ISBN 9781508172505 (library bound)
Subjects: LCSH: Hatshepsut, Queen of Egypt—Juvenile literature. | Egypt—History—Eighteenth dynasty, ca. 1570–1320 B.C.—Juvenile literature. | Pharaohs—Biography—Juvenile literature. | Egypt—Kings and rulers—Biography—Juvenile literature. | Egypt—History—Eighteenth dynasty, ca. 1570–1320 B.C.—Juvenile literature.
Classification: LCC DT87.15 .T45 2017 | DDC 932/.014092 [B] —dc23
LC record available at https://lccn.loc.gov/2016030398

Manufactured in Malaysia

CONTENTS

INTRODUCTION

When we think about the ancient world, we often examine its history through the actions and lives of important leaders. While most of the well-known leaders of yesteryear were men, there have been notable female leaders who transcended the male-dominated civilizations of their time. The emperor known as Hatshepsut was an especially famous and unique ancient Egyptian leader. Perhaps the most incredible aspect of her reign is that she ruled her nation as a king, despite her womanhood.

Archaeologists remain uncertain of the exact dates of her life and reign, but she probably was emperor from either 1504 BCE to 1482 BCE, or from 1479 BCE to 1457 BCE. This was near the beginning of the Egyptian epoch, or era, known as the New Kingdom. What historians and archeologists have uncovered about Hatshepsut has been largely due to the many inscriptions she commissioned. Among these are writings on her memorial temple in western Thebes and in the temple to Amen at Karnak.

Still, little concrete information has survived about her private life. There is even less certainty

This seated statue of Hatshepsut, female pharaoh of Egypt, is a monument to the reign of one of the first female leaders of an ancient civilization.

as to her actual appearance. Unfortunately, many of the documents and records that could have aided us were destroyed by the Egyptians not long after her death, as were many monuments. We do know that her reign marked a time of prosperity, when Egypt thrived. As a daughter, sister, and wife of a pharaoh, she was also the aunt and stepmother of the pharaoh who succeeded her.

Many Egyptologists—those who specialize in ancient Egypt and its artifacts—consider Hatshepsut one of the most successful pharaohs in the civilization's history. Her reign was the longest of any woman who helmed Egypt who came from an indigenous Egyptian line. Egyptologist James Henry Breasted once called her the "first great woman in history of whom we are informed."

Her accomplishments include a variety of successes, especially regarding Egypt's foreign relations. Hatshepsut established important trade relations with regional powers, strengthened Egypt by making peace with its southern neighbors, and built many buildings and other structures throughout both Upper and Lower Egypt.

Until the modern era, there was much confusion about when Hatshepsut actually ruled, whether she was actually a leader or merely a coregent, among many other disagreements. It was only with more recent discoveries, largely uncovered during the late twentieth century, that scholars of all types have been able to discern her true influence and importance as one of the greatest leaders of the ancient world.

CHAPTER 1

THE THUTMOSE DYNASTY

Geography is often a major factor in defining the character and history of nations and peoples. The legacy of Egypt, among the greatest and most influential of ancient civilizations, can hardly be separated from the unique physical conditions that helped bring about its rise.

Egypt is divided into two distinct regions. Upper Egypt, which is actually its southern half, is mostly desert. Cutting through that, however, is a narrow sliver of very fertile land that rests on either side of the mighty Nile river. At about 4,258 miles (6,853 kilometers) long, it is considered the world's longest river.

Rocky mountains lie to the east of the Nile, with desert to its west. Lower Egypt, the nation's northern part, has a flat landscape and is characterized by the Nile delta, where the river divides into smaller branches in the shape of a wide V as it flows out into the Mediterranean Sea.

AN EGYPTIAN DUALITY

This idea of two halves making a whole is a common one in Ancient Egyptian thought, with the country divided into north and south and also into the black fertile land for farming, which was called *kemet*, and the red desert, which was called *deshret*. Egyptian rulers, who are known as pharaohs, were always called the kings of two lands, and the royal headdress was made up of two different crowns, the White Crown of Upper Egypt and the Red Crown of Lower Egypt. The term pharaoh comes from the ancient Egyptian term *per-aa*, or "great house," which was the name of the Egyptian king's palace.

THE HISTORY OF EGYPT

Egyptian history is divided into different periods by scholars in order to make it easier to understand. The first person to do this was an Egyptian priest called Manetho, who wrote a history of Egypt in Greek for the pharaoh Ptolemy I in about 300 BCE.

He divided the kings of Egypt into about thirty different groups, which were called dynasties. The divisions were usually based on different ruling families. Big time periods are also divided, with the main ones called the Old Kingdom (approximately 2600 to 2100 BCE), the Middle Kingdom (approximately 2000 to 1600 BCE) and the New Kingdom (approximately 1550 to 1090 BCE).

RULING EGYPT

The pharaoh was the most powerful member of society, and he was in charge of all religious and political institutions. He selected all the members of the government and all the important priests, who were often members of his own family. The post of king was also considered divine, with the king representing a god called Horus, who was the son of the two important gods Osiris and Isis.

One of the pharaoh's titles was Son of Ra, showing that the king was also closely associated with the sun god Ra. In a spiritual sense, the main role of

This obelisk, one of two of the tapered, four-sided monuments still standing at the Temple of Karnak in Egypt, honors the pharaoh Thutmose I.

the king was to maintain Maat, which is hard to translate exactly but includes the ideas of order and a general sense of rightness and harmony.

During the New Kingdom, the government and administration were based at the capital, Memphis, which was located at the junction between Upper Egypt and Lower Egypt. The religious and ceremonial capital was usually at Thebes in southern (Upper) Egypt. This was the cult center of the god Amen (meaning the Hidden One). Amen became the greatest of all the gods during the New Kingdom, and he was often associated with the most important god of the Old Kingdom, the sun god Ra, to become Amen-Re.

BUILDING AN EMPIRE

The Egyptian Empire encompassed lands to the north and the south. Much of Nubia in the south was governed by an Egyptian viceroy known as the King's Son of Kush. In Syria and Palestine, the situation was more complicated. These areas were made up of small, autonomous states surrounded by larger powers more equal to Egypt, including the Mittanian, Assyrian, and Hittite Empires.

A detail of a sarcophagus, a stone coffin of antiquity, depicts the Egyptian deities Isis and Horus honoring a mummified form of the god Osiris.

The pharaoh allowed the smaller states to retain their own leaders, who were often educated at the Egyptian court. These men were obliged to swear oaths of loyalty to the Egyptian state and to send taxes in the form of food, drink, and other goods. The major powers periodically fought over control of these smaller states. The Egyptian army consisted of a core of full-time soldiers distributed between garrisons in Egypt, Nubia, and Palestine. The pharaoh would conscript additional soldiers for the army from temples and various other government offices when large-scale missions were planned.

THE THUTMOSE DYNASTY

The first pharaoh of the New Kingdom, and the first king of the Eighteenth Dynasty, was called Ahmose I. He ruled from 1550 to 1525 BCE. Ahmose, his brother Kamose, and his father, Seqenenre Ta'a, had fought and defeated the Hyksos, foreign rulers from the northern regions of Canaan and Syria, who had ruled Egypt for about two hundred years. This meant that Ahmose was the first pharaoh in over two hundred years to rule over the whole of a united Egypt.

Ahmose's family came from the city of Thebes, in southern (Upper) Egypt. Although the political capital of Egypt remained Memphis, Thebes became more and more important in the New Kingdom. It was both the cult center of the most important god, Amen, and most of the pharaohs of the New Kingdom chose to be buried nearby in the Valley of the Kings.

AMENHOTEP I

Ahmose died young, probably at about the age of thirty-five, and he was succeeded by his son Amenhotep I, who became the second pharaoh of the Eighteenth Dynasty. At the beginning of his reign in 1525 BCE, Amenhotep was helped by his mother, Ahmose Nefertari, who acted as regent until Amenhotep was old enough to rule by himself. Ahmose Nefertari was also given the title God's Wife of Amen. This meant that she became a priest in charge of some of the religious rituals at the Karnak Temple. The fact that Ahmose Nefertari was given important political and religious duties shows that the governments of the Eighteenth Dynasty did not think it particularly unusual to allow royal women to play significant and powerful roles.

During most of the New Kingdom, the most important god in Egypt was Amen-Re, who was a kind of composite god made up of Amen of Thebes and the sun god Ra. The main temple for worshiping Ra was the impressive Karnak Temple in Thebes.

Amenhotep I was married to his sister Meritamen. We know that they did not have any sons, or at least none who survived childhood. However, they probably did have either a sister or a daughter called Ahmose, although there is some debate among Egyptologists about Ahmose's exact parentage. We know of her existence because the next pharaoh, Thutmose I, based his claim to the throne on the fact that he was her husband.

An archival photo from 1880 shows ruins of the gallery in the second court of Thutmose I, located at the Medinet Habu archaeological site near Luxor, Egypt.

THUTMOSE I

Thutmose I was a middle-aged soldier by the time he became the third pharaoh of the Eighteenth Dynasty and ruler of Egypt in 1504 BCE. He became famous as the first of the great warrior pharaohs of the New Kingdom. He led successful military expeditions south into Nubia and north into Syria, where he left a commemorative stele showing that he had reached as far as the Euphrates River.

One of our main sources of information about the military campaigns conducted by Thutmose I comes from the tomb of a soldier called Ahmose, son of Abana, who lived in a city called El-Kab, about forty miles south of Thebes. The walls of Ahmose's tomb chapel are decorated with something called a tomb autobiography. This is essentially his life story spelled out in pictures and hieroglyphics on the walls of his tomb so that the gods could see how successful he had been in his life and career. We know that in this case the tomb was actually decorated by Ahmose's grandson Paheri, who was a scribe, and on the east wall of the tomb there is a small picture of Paheri standing behind his grandfather.

Ahmose, son of Abana, lived long enough to have been a soldier fighting for four different rulers in succession, and he was a senior military commander under Thutmose I. "I was brave in his presence in the bad water, in the towing of the ship over the cataract. Thereupon I was made crew commander." He describes the northern campaign:

> He [the king] proceeded to Retenu [Syria], to vent his wrath throughout the lands. When his majesty reached Naharin, his majesty found that foe marshalling troops. Then his majesty made a great slaughter of them. Countless were the living captives that his majesty brought back from his victories.

Thutmose I also concentrated on improving the new royal capital at Thebes. He was helped in this by a man called Ineni, who was mayor of Thebes and whose titles included hereditary prince, count, and chief of all works at Karnak. The main list of his achievements comes from his tomb autobiography.

Ineni became superintendent of the king's building projects and was in charge of improvements at Karnak Temple, including the erection of two pylon walls and two obelisks that were nearly 72 feet (22 meters) tall. "I inspected the erection of two obelisks, built the boat of 120 cubits [180 feet, 55 m] in its length, 40 cubits [60 feet, 18 m] in its width, in order to transport these obelisks. They came in peace, safety, and prosperity and landed at Karnak."

An obelisk is a tapering, needlelike stone monument with a minipyramid, or pyramidion, on top. The whole obelisk is usually covered in inscriptions. The pyramidion was often covered in gold leaf in order to reflect the sun, and obelisks were so tall because they were meant to be the first object that the sun's rays fell on in the morning. Obelisks were also meant to represent the first beams of the sun and were an important symbol of worship of the sun god.

FAMILY LIFE OF THE PHARAOH

Thutmose I had two wives, one called Ahmose and another called Mutnofret. It is not clear whether he was married to both women at the same time or if Ahmose became his second wife after the death of his first.

Thutmose had three sons with Mutnofret, called Wadjmose, Amenmose, and Thutmose, and at least two daughters with his wife Ahmose, called Hatshepsut and Neferubity. Neferubity died when she was little more than a baby. Amenmose and Wadjmose both lived until their teenage years. Amenmose was briefly called great army commander, which indicates that he was crown prince and heir to the throne. However, he died young, leaving the third son, Thutmose, as heir.

Hatshepsut and her brothers lived in a separate women's palace with their mothers, other female relations, and many servants. We know that Hatshepsut was particularly fond of her nurse, who was called Sitre and known as Inet, because Hatshepsut later commissioned a statue of herself as queen sitting on her nurse's knee, to be placed in her memorial temple.

New Kingdom royal palaces were known as harem palaces. These consisted of a small village settled within a surrounding wall built of mud bricks. Inside the wall there were gardens full of trees, flowers, fruits and vegetables, and ponds or sometimes even small lakes where people could sit by the water to cool off during the hot weather.

BURYING THE DEAD

During the Old and Middle Kingdoms, pharaohs had been buried in pyramid complexes in the north of the country, either in the Necropolis near the capital at Memphis or slightly farther south near the Faiyum, which was closer to the Middle Kingdom capital at Itj-Tawy.

Hatshepsut's father King Thutmose I died in 1492 BCE, and he was the first Egyptian pharaoh to be buried in a tomb in the Valley of the Kings. The Valley of the

The Valley of the Kings, adjacent to Thebes, is one of biggest and most important burial sites for ancient Egyptian leaders.

Kings is a remote and bleak valley in the rocky mountains that lie to the west of the Nile River at Thebes. Ineni, the mayor of Thebes, who was also in charge of this project, recorded in his own tomb that "I inspected the excavation of the cliff-tomb of his majesty, alone, no one seeing, no one hearing."

The big disadvantage of being buried under a pyramid was that everyone knew where the body was. Throughout Egyptian history, and especially at times of social instability, royal tomb robbery was a major problem for the Egyptian state. Everybody knew that a king or a queen was buried with masses of gold, jewelry, and precious goods. These riches were not just buried in the tomb but also wrapped on and around the monarch's body. In fact, practically every royal burial site has been broken into and robbed, usually quite soon after burial.

Egyptian priests and government officials tried to guard against this, but they often had to reenter tombs in order to clean up the mess that robbers had made. There they would see not just that all the precious goods had been stolen, but sometimes also that the body of the dead person had been literally pulled apart or burned in the effort to find all the treasures that were buried in the wrappings.

Consequently, at the beginning of the New Kingdom, the system of royal burial changed. First, kings and their families were no longer buried in pyramid complexes. They were usually buried near Thebes, in

(SIDEBAR CONTINUED ON THE NEXT PAGE)

(SIDEBAR CONTINUED FROM THE PREVIOUS PAGE)

the south, rather than in the north. This was mainly because the ruling family of the Eighteenth Dynasty came from the south and obviously were more attached both to their own region and also to the place where their own ancestors were buried. Second, the design of the royal tomb complex became two separate structures. The tomb itself was hidden. The memorial temple, which used to be part of the pyramid complex, became a separate building in a different place. Here the priests could perform the rituals involved in the cult of the dead king.

These complexes usually also included a separate kitchen, a bakery for bread and a brewery for making beer, and an area where animals were butchered. There were also rows of storerooms which are now known as magazines.

The royal family actually lived in a separate building within the royal compound. This usually consisted of a square structure enclosing at least one central courtyard. This courtyard was often open to the sky, with a shallow pond in the middle. Rooms would open out all around this central area.

These included a large sitting room, sometimes with a special raised seat built into the wall at one end where the owner would sit, and benches for visitors built against the sides of the other walls.

Bedrooms sometimes had a special bed platform built of mud brick. Otherwise, people slept on wooden beds with webbing across the middle to make them comfortable. There were bathrooms containing a bath or a shower and a toilet. There were also many sets of stairs leading to the roof of the building.

In a country like Egypt, with a warm climate and little rain, many of the day's activities took place outside. Roof spaces would have sunshades or canopies built onto them, and this is often where people had lunch or rested in the afternoon heat. There would have been dozens of servants including nurses, maids, cooks, cleaners, and gardeners. There were also officials, with titles such as overseer of the harem, to ensure that all ran smoothly.

Although Hatshepsut's brothers were taught reading and writing, there is no evidence that royal girls ever went to school. We do not know if Hatshepsut was ever able to read or understand hieroglyphics or hieratic writing, which is the handwritten version of the same language. Nevertheless, as well as having their own nurses, princesses also had their own male tutors, and so there is reason to believe Hatshepsut may well have learned at least basic reading and writing skills.

However, Hatshepsut was certainly trained in the skills considered necessary for the queen of Egypt, as she was the obvious candidate to marry whichever of her brothers would become the next king. Her grandmother and mother had both been given the important priest's title God's Wife of Amen, and she learned all about the rituals and religious duties of this position, as well as the importance and purpose of such ceremonies. In theory, the person appointed as

God's Wife of Amen would go to the great sanctuary of Amen every day. She and the high priest of Amen would ritually destroy effigies (small models) of the

Three sisters are shown in this detail from an ancient mural, and provide a glimpse at more traditional representations of women in Egyptian art.

god's enemies, bathe in the Sacred Lake next to the temple, and prepare food and drink for the statue of the god.

Egyptian children are often shown naked in paintings, but we do not know how often this was the case in real life. When she was a small child, Hatshepsut may have played with no clothes on and also might have been nude on special occasions. However, there are also many actual examples in museums of clothing from ancient Egypt. These clothes are often beautifully and skillfully made out of very fine linen, which comes from the flax plant. We know that the Egyptians could make very beautiful and fine material, with tiny pleating or color ful woven borders with patterns of flowers or birds. Clothes found in the tomb of the pharaoh Tutankhamen, who died when he was about eighteen years old, include some pieces decorated with beads or metalwork. In addition to his shirts, kilts, and tunics, he also had shoes, belts, scarves, hats, and gloves.

Hatshepsut would have usually worn a simple shift dress. This was formed from a tube of material with two straps over the shoulders, and in the winter long sleeves were attached to the straps.

Her sandals were made of reeds woven and plaited together or from fine leather. Her hair was worn in a thick braid on the right side of her head. She had many hair slides and decorations made of gold, silver, and precious jewels, as well as other pieces of jewelry, including bracelets, anklets, earrings, and necklaces. Sometimes, on special occasions, Hatshepsut may also have worn an overdress made entirely of small beads strung together, and there are a couple of examples of such dresses in museums today. Her toys included balls and model animals, and she also had both wooden and cloth dolls, some with many changes of clothing for dressing up.

CHAPTER 2

HATSHEPSUT AND KING THUTMOSE II

In 1492 BCE, Thutmose's only surviving heir, Thutmose II, succeeded his father. On the day of his coronation, the new pharaoh received five "great names." These were supposed to reflect his character, interests, reputation, lineage, or other elements of his persona. In written Egyptian hieroglyphics, the prenomen and and the nomen—the last two names of the king—were enclosed in decorative ovals known as cartouches. These designated the names as royal. The king's formal name, the prenomen, was used in matters such as foreign affairs, and as part of official statements. His family and friends used his personal name, the more informal nomen.

Thutmose chose Aakheperenre ("Becomes Great like Ra") and Thutmose ("Thoth is born"), which was probably the name he was known by while growing up.

Thutmose probably retained Thoth as he was the god of writing and knowledge. Thoth was also closely associated with the moon. Thutmose II was almost certainly already married to his half sister Hatshepsut by the time he came to the throne. His reign began in traditional fashion, with his wife, Hatshepsut, acting as his queen. Modern estimates vary as to how old they were at the time of their accession, but most historians agree they were probably both teenagers.

Although a rather shadowy figure in Egyptian history, we know that Thutmose II continued with his father's military policies, with campaigns in both Nubia to the south and Syria to the north. We know, for example, that there was a revolt against Egyptian rule in Nubia during the first year of his reign. Official records state:

> One came to inform his majesty as follows: "The vile Kush [Nubia] has begun to rebel, those who were the subjects of the Lord of the Two Lands had planned hostility, beginning to smite him." His majesty was furious at the news, like a panther, when he heard it.

These heiroyglyphics adorn the walls of the tomb of Thutmose II, in the Valley of the Kings.

Thutmose decided that firm action was needed to suppress this rebellion, and the Egyptians were ruthless against the Nubians. Official historians recorded:

> His majesty dispatched a numerous army into Nubia . . . in order to overthrow all those who were rebellious against his majesty . . . This army of his majesty overthrew those barbarians. They did not let live anyone among their males, according to the command of his majesty, except one of those children of the chief of Kush, who was taken away alive as a living prisoner to his majesty.

Bringing back the son of the Nubian chieftain to be educated and trained in Egypt, perhaps with the idea of eventually sending him back to Nubia to rule as a vassal, is an example of the policy introduced by the Thutmose pharaohs. Young men from foreign royal or government families were brought to Egypt in order to educate them about the Egyptian way of life.

We know that Thutmose II also conducted at least one successful military campaign in Syria.

Another tomb autobiography at the cemetery in El-Kab, this time belonging to a soldier called Ahmose-Penekhbet, records, "I followed King Aakheperenre triumphant, there were brought for me in Bedouin Land very many living prisoners, I did not count them." There is also a small fragment of an inscription in a temple at Deir el-Bahri that lists the gifts (or, more likely, the spoils of war) that Thutmose II managed to get in Syria, including elephants.

Thutmose II was also interested in continuing the building projects started by his father, although little evidence remains of which buildings were commissioned or completed by him. Once more, mayor Ineni of Thebes was the one in charge of these projects. "I was a favorite of the king in his every place . . . I attained the old age of the revered, I possessed the favor of his majesty every day, I was supplied from the table of the king."

Hatshepsut acted as queen and partner to Thutmose II. She was given the titles King's Daughter, King's Sister, and King's Great Wife, all of which were true. She also became God's Wife of Amen, and it was this title that she was most proud of and used most often in inscriptions. Thutmose II and

Hatshepsut had one daughter together who was named Neferure. Thutmose also had a son with his secondary wife, Isis, who was also called Thutmose.

Two tombs were now begun for the royal couple. The tomb for Thutmose II was begun in the Valley of the Kings. As there wasn't yet a special cemetery for royal women, Hatshepsut chose to have her tomb constructed in the cliffs facing the river opposite the city at Thebes. A large, yellow stone sarcophagus was placed in the tomb, and it was inscribed, "The Great Princess, great in favor and grace, Mistress of All the Lands, Royal Daughter and Royal Sister, God's Wife, Great Royal Wife, Mistress of the Two Lands, Hatshepsut." However, when this tomb was excavated by archaeologist Howard Carter in 1916, he found that the construction work had never been finished and that the tomb had obviously never been used.

BECOMING QUEEN REGENT

The next ruler of Egypt was the next royal male heir, and this was Thutmose II's son by his secondary wife, Isis. The boy was probably younger than ten years old at the time of his father's death, but nonetheless he was proclaimed King of Upper and Lower Egypt, Menkheperre, Son of Ra, Thutmose III.

Where did this leave Hatshepsut? She was at that time about thirty years of age. Her father and brother were both dead. She had been both the daughter of a pharaoh and the wife of a pharaoh. She was both aunt and stepmother to the new boy king. Although she was still young, it was unthinkable that she could remarry and have another family. After all, who would be a suitable husband for such a powerful woman? Also, any husband would then be in a powerful position to try to take over the throne of Egypt.

As had happened earlier in the Eighteenth Dynasty when a child came to the throne, Hatshepsut was now called upon to act as regent for the young pharaoh. This meant that she was expected to use all of her experience to help him rule until he was old enough to manage by himself.

However, this was the first time that a queen had been asked to act as regent for someone who was not her own child, but rather the offspring of her husband and another woman, a less important and much less royal woman. In fact, Hatshepsut could claim much more royal blood in her veins than the present ruler could. Her problem was that she was a woman, and a woman couldn't be pharaoh.

We have no evidence as to what Hatshepsut's private feelings were, and for the first few years of Thutmose III's reign she fulfilled all the

This wall painting of farmers using cows to trample wheat is one of many images decorating the tomb of Menna, also known as TT69.

duties of a queen regent. In the second year of Thutmose III's reign, for example, a temple was finished at Semna in Nubia. This temple replaced a temple first built there during the Middle Kingdom. It was dedicated to the memory of the Middle Kingdom pharaoh Senwosret III and also to a Nubian god called Dedwen.

An inscription in the temple, under a picture of Dedwen embracing Thutmose III, supposedly repeats words said by the god himself. It reads, "My beloved son Menkheperre, how beautiful is this beautiful monument, which you have made for my beloved son the King of Upper and Lower Egypt, Khakaure (Senwosret III). You have perpetuated his name forever." Note that there is no thanks given to Hatshepsut, and indeed she is hardly mentioned at all in the temple.

THE QUEEN REGENT

There are some clues that Hatshepsut may have acted more like a king than was perhaps expected from a regent. An inscription from the tomb of mayor Ineni, who by that time had served under three Thutmose kings and was a very old man, reads, "His son stood in his place as king of the Two Lands, having become ruler upon the throne of the one who begat him. His sister the Divine Consort, Hatshepsut, governed the land and the Two Lands were under her control. Egypt was made to labor with bowed head for her."

Another clue is found in an inscription on a building now known as the Red Chapel. This was once a large building that Hatshepsut had made to house the bark of the god Amen at Karnak. The bark was a small wooden boat covered in gold that was used to transport the statue of a god. There are many illustrations on the temple walls of priests carrying such barks though the temples and streets of Thebes during religious festivals.

The Red Chapel is so called because it was made out of blocks of a red quartz stone, and the whole building was covered in inscriptions describing events during the reign of Hatshepsut. Unfortunately for modern scholars, at some point after the death of Hatshepsut, Thutmose III had the building demolished, and for thousands of years the blocks were hidden as filling and foundations for other walls. They were discov-

THE TOMBS OF THUTMOSE II

This wall painting of farmers using cows to trample wheat is one of many images decorating the tomb of Menna, also known as TT 69. In 1479 BCE, Thutmose II died. It remains uncertain which tomb in the Valley of the Kings was intended for him. It may have been an almost undecorated tomb known today as KV 42 (KV stands for King's Valley). This is because toward the end of the New Kingdom, many of the royal tombs were broken into and robbed. Consequently, during the third intermediate period about 500 years after the death of Thutmose II, many of the royal mummies were removed and hidden together in a combined tomb near Deir el- Bahri. When these were discovered in 1881, the mummies were shipped down the Nile to the main museum at Cairo.

Thutmose II was unwrapped in 1886 by the French Egyptologist Gaston Maspero, who found Thutmose's body badly damaged by tomb robbers. Both his arms and one of his legs had been broken off and then had been bandaged back into place. Maspero did note that Thutmose II was about five feet, six inches (168 centimeters) tall, with thinning hair and a bald patch.

ered in the 1950s and the building has recently been rebuilt and is now visible once more on the grounds of the Karnak Temple.

One inscription on the walls of this chapel describes a religious festival at the neighboring Luxor Temple held in the second year of Thutmose III's reign. This festival usually included a ritual in which the god of the Luxor Temple helped the king to reaffirm his royal status and

The sarcophagus of Hatshepsut was commissioned by her, but she then had it recut for her father, Thutmose I. She later had his mummy transferred into it.

his unity with his royal spirit, or *ka*. Apparently on this occasion the festival didn't quite go according to plan, as the god decided to make an extra announcement.

Hatshepsut describes what happened: "A great oracle in the presence of this good god, proclaiming for me the kingship of the two lands, Upper and Lower Egypt being under the fear of me, in Year 2 . . . the third day of the festival of Amen . . . being the ordination of the two lands for me."

This has been interpreted to mean that Hatshepsut and the current pharaoh were told together that she was heir to the throne and would be the next ruler of Egypt. The inscription is not dated, and there is debate among archaeologists as to which year it was, and

Mummification is most strongly identified with Egypt. The mummified form of Thutmose IV shown here gives us a good idea of what he might have truly looked like in life.

This portrait of Hatshepsut, unlike some other well known representations, plays up a more feminine image of the pharaoh.

whether the king in question was Thutmose I, II, or III. It is impossible to know whether this event ever took place, or which king was with her at the time, but it is an interesting indication that Hatshepsut was not afraid of using the gods of Egypt to back her up with any future claim to the throne.

As far as we can tell, the next few years of the reign of Thutmose III passed uneventfully. However, Hatshepsut was secretly becoming more and more dissatisfied with her behind-the-scenes role. She gradually worked to obtain a greater role in ruling the country, and by the end of 1473 BCE, in the seventh year that Thutmose III had been pharaoh, Hatshepsut was crowned as the joint king of Egypt.

CHAPTER 3

HATSHEPSUT THE KING

Even before new evidence had been uncovered in the late twentieth century, scholars had been divided and generally unclear about Hatshepsut's rule. One major bone of contention among experts has been how, exactly, a woman came to power at the time. Jean Francois Champollion, a nineteenth century pioneer in Egyptology from France and the first to decipher hieroglyphs, initially assumed that Hatshepsut must have been a man.

By the beginning of the twentieth century, however, Egyptologists did not have trouble accepting that Hatshepsut had ruled as a woman. At this point, of course, Queen Victoria had ruled Britain successfully for many years. These archaeologists thought of the pharaoh Hatshepsut in a similar vein, as a wise, motherly woman who spread peace and prosperity throughout her empire.

In the last hundred years, though, opinions about her have been widely divided. Some people think that she was an evil schemer who used sexual favors to sleep her way to the throne. Others assume that she was a wicked stepmother who stole the throne from her poor, defenseless stepson.

We do not know what Hatshepsut's reasons were for working to proclaim herself king, although fierce personal ambition obviously played an important part. We can only really judge her from the events and actions that we do know about, and it is generally acknowledged that her reign as pharaoh of Egypt was very successful. Egypt prospered under her rule, with many beautiful and elaborate buildings constructed throughout her reign. She also ordered a number of adventurous trading missions that traveled long distances away from Egypt and returned with many exotic foreign goods. Egyptian territories in Nubia to the south and the Levant in the northeast were successfully defended during her reign.

Hatshepsut's rise to the throne gradually gained pace during the early years of her regency. For some years, she had been an important priestess in temple rituals at Thebes as part of her role

This statue head of Hatshepsut from the Neues Museum in Berlin, Germany, sports the fake beard the pharaoh queen wore in homage to Osiris, much like the male pharaohs.

as God's Wife of Amen. Shortly before her rise to the throne, she also took on the ritual of making offerings directly to the gods, a ritual usually reserved for the pharaoh alone. It is also known that while she was still regent, she commissioned various important building works, again something that was usually only ordered, and paid for, by the pharaoh. These actions suggest that she was reinforcing her own authority and her right to the throne by showing herself to others performing kinglike duties.

It is also the case that she could only have become pharaoh with the agreement, if not the active support, of the men in charge of the day-to-day running of the government. These included the heads of the army, the chief priests of Amen and the important state temples, and those men in charge of the civil service. Many of these officials, including Ineni, mayor of Thebes, and the soldier Ahmose-Penekhbet, had lived through the reigns of Thutmose I and Thutmose II, and they seemed happy to accept Hatshepsut's new position.

When Hatshepsut was regent, she chose carefully the men who were promoted to important positions. Such people may then have felt that their positions were due to her favor, and that their good fortunes were linked with hers. Consequently, it would have been in their interest to support her rise to power. Hatshepsut appointed a new chief priest or First Prophet of Amen called Hapuseneb, and also promoted a man called Senenmut, who had been appointed Steward of the God's Wife and Steward of the King's Daughter by Thutmose II and was also the tutor to Hatshepsut's daughter, Neferure.

Senenmut came from a large, educated family in Armant, which is about fifteen miles south of Thebes. After Hatshepsut became king, Senenmut was promoted to Overseer of All Royal Works and Steward of Amen. He was a very competent official and for many years he seems to have acted as Hatshepsut's closest adviser. Some modern scholars have assumed that he was also Hatshepsut's secret lover, but there is no evidence for this. Neferure was also promoted to the position of God's Wife of Amen.

HATSHEPSUT'S CORONATION

There are no records that describe the day of Hatshepsut's coronation. This is because for the rest of

Senenmut, chief advisor and architect of Hatshepsut, is portrayed in this quartzite statue holding the pharaoh's daugher, Princess Neferure.

her reign she sometimes liked to pretend that she came to power straight after the death of her father, Thutmose I, and at other times she counted her reign from the time of the death of her husband-brother, Thutmose II. Consequently it was not really in her interest to commission inscriptions that specified when exactly she came to the throne.

An important part of Hatshepsut's coronation was the selection of her royal names. These were used by every pharaoh as symbols to reinforce their claim to the throne. The names defined their relationship to the gods of Egypt and also to the land itself. It was obviously particularly important for Hatshepsut to stress her claim to the throne with her own names. Hatshepsut's nomen, or Daughter of Ra name, now became Khnum-Amen Hatshepsut.

A later inscription on the wall of Hatshepsut's temple at Deir el-Bahri describes a fictional scene in which her father, Thutmose I, and the sun god Ra reveal her other royal names. The inscription reads:

> His majesty commanded the lector priests to be brought to inscribe her great names at the moment of receiving her insignia of King of

> Upper and Lower Egypt . . . They then inscribed her names of King of Upper and Lower Egypt. Indeed the god inspired their minds to compile her names exactly as he had compiled them first; Her Great Name The Horus Powerful of Kas, Her Great Name She of Two Ladies Flourishing in Years, Her Great Name Horus of Gold She of Divine Risings, Her Great Name King of Upper and Lower Egypt Maatkare, given life eternally.

PREPARING HER TOMB

Hatshepsut decided that the best place to be buried was in the same tomb as her father, Thutmose I. Thutmose I's tomb, now known as KV 20, had been completed some years before. Hatshepsut re-opened the tomb and embarked on extensive alterations.

The tomb had originally consisted of a long single corridor leading to a large burial chamber. A new entrance was hacked into the back of the

A MEMORIAL TEMPLE

Now that Hatshepsut was pharaoh, she turned her attention to one of the most important tasks facing any new ruler of Egypt—the preparation of her own memorial temple, where her spirit, or ka, would be protected forever, and the construction of a tomb fit for a king.

Hatshepsut chose a location for her memorial temple in a natural bay near the Theban mountains, today called Deir el-Bahri, which was an area already famous both as a cult center for the goddess Hathor and as the location of the tomb of the first Middle Kingdom ruler, called Nebhepetre Monthuhotep.

The site also faced the entrance to the important Amen-Re Temple at Karnak on the other side of the river. Her cliff-face tomb was now abandoned, and Hatshepsut looked for a suitable site in the best, most royal, venue—the Valley of the Kings. Hapuseneb, the Chief Priest of Amen, was put in charge of building the tomb, and Senenmut, whom she had appointed the Overseer of all Royal Works, was in charge of construction work at Deir el-Bahri.

burial chamber, where a staircase was to lead down to a new burial hall carved out of the rock. This hall contained three centrally aligned pillars and three storage rooms off to the side. The stone of the hill-side here was rather crumbly shale, and so instead of painting decorations straight onto the walls, large limestone blocks were brought down to line the sides of the room. These were decorated with scenes from the Book of Amduat, which describes the Egyptian idea of the underworld.

The burial chamber also contained two large, yellow quartzite sarcophagi, one for the body of Hatshepsut and one for her father, Thutmose I. After the alterations were finished, the body of Thutmose was then moved downstairs and placed in his grand new stone coffin, and Hatshepsut planned to be buried next to him. This is not the end of the story, however, for several years after the death of Hatshepsut, Thutmose III reopened the tomb and took away the body of his grandfather, placing it instead in a new specially built tomb (KV 38) elsewhere in the Valley of the Kings. The present whereabouts of the body of Thutmose I are unknown, although he may be one of the unidentified bodies from the group of royal mummies found near Deir el-Bahri.

A PLACE AMONG THE GODS

Hathor was an important goddess who was sometimes shown as a woman and sometimes as a cow. One of her main roles was divine mother of each ruling king. She was also associated with funerary beliefs, especially at Thebes, where she was also known as Goddess of the West. Since at least the time of the Middle Kingdom, the site of Deir el-Bahri was associated with Hathor, and it is possible that the association with such a powerful goddess influenced Hatshepsut to choose this as the location for her own memorial temple. This

This is but one section of the system of ruins—including many temples and tombs—that make up the Karnak Temple Complex in Luxor, Egypt.

was going to be the cult center for her own ka after she died. It was also the place where the king was worshiped as a god. In theory it would stand for eternity, so that she would never be forgotten and could exist for eternity in the afterlife. In an ordinary cult temple, a single sanctuary or shrine for the image of a god would be built in the innermost, secret part of the building. In a memorial temple, the emphasis was different.

The basic plan of New Kingdom memorial temples followed a specific pattern, which is visible in Hatshepsut's temple. As well as celebrating the cult of the dead king, another major function of the temple was to identify the king with particular gods, especially Osiris, Ra, and Amen. From the Old Kingdom onward, the king had been compared with the god Horus while alive and after his death with the god Osiris. In a sense each dead king became one with Osiris. Sanctuaries to Osiris tended to be dark, secret places and were often built on the left side of the temple. Another funerary belief dating from the Old Kingdom was to compare the living king with the sun god Ra, or a combined version of two sun gods called Ra-Harakhty. Sanctuaries to this god tended to have an area containing an altar open to the sky, and were usually placed on the right side of the temple.

Amen was the most important god of the New Kingdom, making him the most important god for the the king and the country. The sanctuary for Amen was usually placed in the middle of the back of the temple. A chapel for the dead king was also located on the left near or with the Osiris sanctuary, and there was also a false door stele at the back where offerings of food and drink were made to feed the ka of the dead king.

DJESER DJESERU

The temple of Hatshepsut is known today as one of the most beautiful buildings in Egypt. The temple was called Djeser Djeseru, which means "holiest of the holy." This name implied that the monument was the best of the best. It took fifteen years to build. The architect may have been Senenmut. One of his titles was controller of the works at Djeser Djeseru. Others certainly contributed to the project, including the chief treasurer called Djehuty, who claimed, "I led the craftsmen to work in the works of Djeser Djeseru."

The temple was constructed next to the earlier Middle Kingdom temple built by Nebhepetre Monthuhotep, and to some extent it copies the same design. Both temples were designed to blend into the surrounding scenery and to look as if they were growing out of the hillside. The memorial temple was designed on multiple levels and consists of three broad courts separated by colonnades, which are linked by ascending ramps. The first building of the complex (now lost) was a small temple built by an architect called Puimre and was located on the bank of a canal leading into the desert. An

Located at Deir el-Bahri, the vast Mortuary Temple of Hatshepsut is one of the most distinctive structures in the region.

avenue 121 feet (37 meters) wide and lined on both sides with sphinxes having the body of a lion and the head of Hatshepsut led from this temple across the valley floor to an enormous pylon gateway (also now lost).

ENTERING THE TEMPLE

This gateway led to the first open courtyard of the temple, which was described by Hatshepsut as "a garden for my father Amen." A series of shallow, circular pits in the ground shows that this garden was once filled with beautiful trees and shrubs imported from Punt. There was a wide-roofed corridor at the back of this courtyard, with eleven stone pillars holding up the roof on either side of an enormous ramp in the middle. Two huge statues of Hatshepsut as Osiris, with her body wrapped in a tight-fitting cloak and with her arms crossed on her chest, were visible. The ramp led up to the second courtyard. This was another large, open space with a covered portico and a large ramp to the rear. A chapel dedicated to Hathor is off to the south side, and a chapel dedicated to Anubis, the jackal-headed god of embalming, is on the north side.

The central ramp led up to the third, or upper, terrace. Here there was a roofed portico that originally had a row of standing figures of Hatshepsut in front of each of the columns. A large, pink granite doorway in the middle led to a courtyard circled by columns on all four sides. On the south side of this court a corridor led to a chapel dedicated to Osiris and the royal cult of Hatshepsut and her father. There was also a chapel with a small, open court and an altar to the sun god Ra-Harakhty on the north. Cut into the rock at the very back of the temple was a shrine to the god Amen. This temple is a great source of information about the life and reign of Hatshepsut, as almost all the walls of the temple are covered with illustrations of important events from her reign. There are also many religious scenes of Hatshepsut with various gods.

Sadly, the temple has suffered much damage over the course of history. Toward the end of the reign of Thutmose III, Hatshepsut's name and most of the representations of her were carefully chiseled out. Most of the images of the gods, especially the god Amen, were also chiseled out during the reign of the pharaoh Akhenaten. Though the images of these gods were recarved after his death, the pictures of Hatshepsut were not. During the Nineteenth Dynasty, Rameses II ordered the destruction of all the Osiris statues. Finally, in the seventh century AD, early Christians, known as Copts, disapproved of graven images and defaced the features of the remaining gods. Consequently, when the burial site was first excavated by Edouard Naville in 1891, it was little more than a ruin. However, a team of Polish archaeologists began work restoring the temple in 1961, and it is now fully restored and completely open to the public.

OBELISKS: GIFTS TO THE GODS

Even before becoming pharaoh, Hatshepsut had ordered two obelisks from the granite quarries at Aswan. During the New Kingdom, obelisks became popular cult objects. They were often erected in temples in pairs against the front of pylon gateways. They were gifts from the king to the sun god, and their tall shafts contained columns of hieroglyphs describing the erection and the particular ceremonies and prayers involved. Obelisks were also sometimes regarded as objects of worship in their own right, and people prayed to them and even gave them names.

One statue from the Mortuary Temple of Hateshepsut is shown up close, the colossus of the pharaoh herself.

Thutmose I and Ineni had erected two obelisks at Karnak Temple, and Hatshepsut wanted to follow her father's example. Indeed, an inscription on one of her obelisks claims that "Your father, the King of Upper and Lower Egypt, gave a command to erect obelisks." Hatshepsut was obviously very proud of commissioning and erecting these huge religious objects. The story of the expedition to Aswan to bring the stones back to Karnak Temple is told both on the walls of her Red Chapel and on the back wall of the first courtyard of her memorial temple. Cutting out, moving, and erecting obelisks represents an incredible feat of engineering and organization even by today's standards. Remember that the Egyptians had no machinery to help them, and every stage of the operation was achieved by hand alone. The reason that they were able to do these things is that the Egyptians were very good at organizing people. There were always hundreds if not thousands of workers available, and everybody understood that projects of this type could take a long time to complete.

In order to cut out a granite obelisk, rows of men would sit on the ground and pound small balls of a hard stone called dolerite against the surface of the rock. This gradually produced a channel in the rock. Once the channels were deep enough, the two teams of men then chiseled sideways underneath the obelisk in order to carve the obelisk out. We know that a second pair of obelisks produced later in Hatshepsut's reign took seven months to dig out. Once the stones were free, they were dragged from the quarry to the riverside and loaded onto enormous barges, which would then be pulled downstream to Thebes.

Senenmut was put in charge of the whole obelisk project, and we know that he was sent to Aswan to check that everything was going smoothly. While there he carved an inscription in the quarry which states that he went "In order to inspect the work on the two great obelisks of Heh. It happened just as it was commanded that everything be done, it happened because of the power of her majesty."

The first scene in Hatshepsut's memorial temple shows a large barge with two obelisks tied to the deck being towed by twenty-seven boats, each filled with thirty rowers. Three smaller boats are sailing alongside the barge, and these all contain priests performing religious ceremonies. The accompanying inscriptions suggest that everyone was "sailing down stream with gladness of heart."

The next scene shows the arrival of the barge at Thebes. On one side of the river an enormous group of soldiers is waiting to unload the obelisks, and the inscription above reads that men have been brought from all over Egypt to help with the task. On the other side a group of priests are celebrating the arrival with prayers of thanks. There are also scenes of celebrations in the town, and it is likely that the day was declared a public holiday so that all the residents could come and witness the marvelous event. "The companions, the dignitaries, the officials, the soldiers of the whole land, say 'Happy is your heart, this day has come to pass.' " The bases of these two obelisks are still visible today at Karnak Temple, but sadly the shafts disappeared long ago.

CHAPTER 4

THE FACE OF THE PHARAOH

Now that Hatshepsut had become joint pharaoh, she needed to make a decision. What would her public persona be? It was a different consideration in ancient Egypt than it would be today, and not only because modern people have different opinions about gender equality. Few of Hatshepsut's subject would have any occasion to lay eyes on her at any point in her reign. To most Egyptians, it probably made little difference who ruled over them. They would be content with experiencing peace, plentiful harvests, and being free from flooding and other disasters that occasionally befell them.

There was no mass media; no television, radio, or newspaper; and very little information about what was happening in the court would ever have reached the common people or affected what happened to them. It should also be remembered that most people could not read. In such a society, with very low levels of literacy, the best way to pass on information was through pictures.

Egypt was a religious society, and most people had small, personal altars or shrines to gods in their houses. They also went to local town and village temples for religious services, and, occasionally, on special occasions or during religious festivals, all

A close-up relief of a part of the Roman Temple of Deir el-Hagar, in the Western Desert region near Dahkla Oasis, Egypt, shows the common motif of the bird.

the large temples throughout the country opened their doors to the population.

The people weren't actually allowed to venture very far inside these temples, but they certainly stood outside the front pylon gateways, which were covered in pictures. We also know that at Karnak they were allowed a little way into the temple, because one of the outer courtyards is called the court of the multitude. There are also examples of a hieroglyphic bird sign called a *rekhyt* carved onto the walls of the temple that represents the people of Egypt and indicates where they were allowed to stand there. Consequently, throughout the New Kingdom, pharaohs had images and statues of themselves placed in temples throughout the country.

REPRESENTATIONS OF HATSHEPSUT

During her time as wife of Thutmose II and as regent for Thutmose III, Hatshepsut had always been represented in such images as a conventional Egyptian princess and wife. However, the situation changed. The statues that she commissioned at the beginning of her reign still show her with a female face and body but wearing the traditional clothes of a male king, including a short kilt, a broad collar, a crown, a *nemes* headcloth, and a false beard. The nemes headcloth was a piece of striped cloth pulled tight across the forehead and tied at the back of the neck with two flaps on either side of the face. The false beard was another symbol of the divine nature of kingship and was a plaited beard often depicted as blue (like lapis lazuli) and tied onto the king's chin by a piece of cord.

Although these statues were not actual portraits in the sense that we think of them today, they do give some clues as to what Hatshepsut may have looked like. She had an oval face with almond-shaped eyes, a rather big nose, and a small chin. Her statues also sometimes show that she had high, arching eyebrows.

We also know she was quite vain. One of the stories carved onto the walls of her temple at Deir el-Bahri is a detailed representation of her conception and birth, with the god Amen as her father. The text also includes a description of her growing up: "Her majesty grew beyond everything; to look upon her was more beautiful than anything . . . her form was like a god . . . her majesty was a maiden, beautiful, blooming."

Soon after her seventh year as regent, this style of representation was abandoned. From then on, Hatshepsut chose to be represented as a man both in statues and in illustrations on temple walls. Most likely this was because it was thought to be confusing, uncomfortable, and against tradition for people to think that their pharaoh was actually a woman. It was easier to just show her as a man.

There is no indication that anyone who knew about her was actually fooled by this. Indeed, many of the inscriptions that accompany male images of Hatshepsut still refer to her as a woman, or use feminine endings for words describing her. Interesting examples of this confusion include two identical sphinxes originally from the avenue leading to Djeser Djeseru. One, now in the Cairo Museum, is inscribed "Maatkare, beloved of Amen, may he be given life for ever." Another, now in the Metropolitan Museum in New York, is inscribed "Maatkare, beloved of Amen, may she be given life for ever."

A sphinx was a mythical creature usually made up of the body of a lion and the head of a human. From the Old Kingdom onward, statues of pharaohs as sphinxes had been used to represent the pharaoh's royalness and strength. They also

Many pharaohs had themselves immortalized in sphinx form for posterity. This limestone sphinx of Hatshepsut, resides at Deir el-Bahri.

indicated the fighting nature of the king.

TEMPLE RESTORATION

Sometime after her ninth year as regent (1471 BCE), Hatshepsut decided that she would follow one of the traditions set by her ancestors and begin an ambitious program of construction in Egypt and Nubia. One of her motivations for this was to show everyone in Egypt that the country was in safe hands and nothing had really changed. On the front of one of her temples the boastful inscription reads, "The altars are opened, the sanctuaries are enlarged . . . the desires of all gods; every one is in possession of the dwelling which he has loved, his ka rests upon his throne." The inscription goes on to state, "The lands together are under my authority, the Black [Nile Valley] and the Red [Desert] are under my authority. My fame makes the great ones of the countries to bow down, while the uraeus is upon my forehead." The uraeus was a special symbol of kingship in the form of a rearing snake that protruded just above the forehead in royal crowns and headdresses. This snake represented the goddess Wadjet of Lower Egypt.

A lioness goddess called Pakhet (literally "she who scratches") had been worshiped in an area of Middle Egypt since the Middle Kingdom onward. Hatshepsut built a temple to this goddess at a site known today as Speos Artemidos. Lion-headed goddesses such as Pakhet, Bastet ("she of the city Bast"), Sekhmet ("the powerful"), Matit ("the dismemberer"), and Mehit ("the seizer") were thought of as fierce and dangerous. At the same time, however, they were also worshiped for their childbearing and nurturing instincts. Hatshepsut had already shown a preference for goddesses by choosing to place her memorial temple at a site of special significance to the goddess Hathor, and it is tempting to imagine she was again motivated by a desire to honor a powerful female figure.

AN ERA OF RELATIVE PEACE

There are very few records or inscriptions of any wars during the reign of Hatshepsut. This has led some scholars to believe that, unlike most other New Kingdom pharaohs, she did nothing to protect Egypt or to maintain her empire in Nubia and Syria. However, there is some evidence from her memorial temple that Hatshepsut did take part in campaigns in both regions. One scene shows the Nubian god Dedwen leading a group of captives toward the pharaoh. Another, badly damaged, inscription states that "as was done by her father, the King of Upper and Lower Egypt Aakheperkare, who seized all lands . . . a slaughter was made among them, the number being unknown, their hands were cut off." There is also some evidence that she may have campaigned in Canaan or Syria, from an inscription reading that "her arrow is among the northerners."

Although there is little evidence of her military activities, the fact that none of the foreign areas under Egypt tried to rebel during her reign and that no countries tried to invade Egypt suggests that she did enough to defend her empire successfully. Another indication of Hatshepsut's interest in the army was that Thutmose III was sent off to a military academy to train to become a soldier.

The temple consists of two parts, with an outer, pillared hall connected by a short corridor to an inner sanctuary carved out of the hillside. A series of illustrations are carved on the inner wall of the pillared hall, with a picture of Hatshepsut praying to the god Amen while Pakhet stands behind her saying, "... [M]y fiery breath being as a fire against your enemies."

Hatshepsut also launched a restoration program for temples that had been neglected since the unrest of the second intermediate period. A temple

This fresco, taken from an 1878 atlas of Egyptian art, depicts a princely chariot typical of the Eighteenth Dynasty.

to the goddess Hathor at Cusae, forty miles south of Speos Artemidos, had apparently suffered badly: "The temple of the Mistress of Cusae had begun to fall to ruin, the ground had swallowed up its noble sanctuary, so that the children played on its roof...I adorned it, having been built anew, I overlaid its image with gold."

A THIRTY-YEAR CELEBRATION

In the fifteenth year of her regency (1265 BCE) Hatshepsut celebrated a Heb-Sed Festival. This jubilee celebration of the king's reign was usually first celebrated after a king had been in power for thirty years, and then every three years afterward. It was meant to renew the king's power through a ritual of rebirth and recrowning. It is not clear why Hatshepsut decided to celebrate so early, but the festival was a national celebration enjoyed by everyone. There were five days of national holiday and religious festivals in all the major temples throughout the country, culminating in a grand procession of all the gods.

In theory, as joint pharaoh, Thutmose III was also celebrating, but there is very little evi-

Here is an interior view of an arched chamber in the Temple of Hatshepsut at Karnak.

dence of his involvement apart from a few illustrations on the walls of Djeser Djeseru, where both kings are pictured making offerings together.

Hatshepsut commissioned another pair of obelisks for the Karnak Temple to mark the celebrations. Senenmut was once more in charge of the project. He chose a granite quarry at Sehek near Aswan run by a man called Amenhotep, who later described himself as "The real confidant of the King, his beloved, the director of the work on the two big obelisks, the chief priest of Khnum, Satis, and Anukis, Amen ho tep." Rather than putting the obelisks in front of a pylon gateway, Hatshepsut chose instead to place them in the middle of a hypostyle hall built by her father, Thutmose I. Unfortunately this meant that she had to demolish the southern wall and remove many columns as well as the roof in order to fit them in.

Both obelisks had single columns of inscriptions running down all four faces, and extra inscriptions were added around each base. The vertical inscriptions listed all of Hatshepsut's titles and then affirmed that all the gods were pleased with her. The inscriptions around the bases are more informative. Here Hatshepsut tells the story of how and why she had the monuments made. "I did it for him in fidelity of heart, as a king to every god. It was my desire to make them for him." She was obviously very proud of her achievement, and another inscription reads, "These two great obelisks, which my majesty has had made with electrum [gold leaf] for my father Amen, in order that my name shall last, enduring in this

This relief from the red chapel at the Temple of Hatshepsut shows hieroglyphs representing a gift of wine to the pharaoh.

temple for ever and ever, they are of one block of enduring granite without seam or joining."

Hatshepsut also made other additions to Karnak Temple. Her Red Chapel was installed in the innermost part of the temple, and this was surrounded by a small group of other chapels covered in inscriptions of Hatshepsut making offerings to various gods. She also improved the processional way between the shrine of Amen and that of his goddess wife Mut, and added various stops along the route for the sacred bark. Her other major addition was a new pylon gateway, now known as pylon VIII. This was decorated with scenes of her father discussing her with the gods Amen, Mut, and Khonsu. It shows Thutmose praying for the success of her reign. He says, "I come to you, lord of the gods, I pray before you, in return for this you have put the Black and the Red Land under the rule of my daughter, the King of Upper and Lower Egypt, Maatkare." This inscription reinforces the idea that Hatshepsut is the rightful ruler, and that her father and the gods recognize her right to be pharaoh.

CHAPTER 5

AN AGE OF COMMERCE AND DISCOVERY

The reign of Hatshepsut was also marked by an interest in the outside world, beyond Egypt's immediate borders. This included exploring far afield as well as attempting to establish trade with other nations and peoples. Historians say that the pharaoh dispatched representatives to obtain turquoise from the distant mountains of the Sinai peninsula, as well as trade expeditions to buy cedarwood in Lebanon. The former route was a difficult, overland trip through the desert to the Red Sea, where ships would take the traders to the west coast of Sinai.

In the sixteenth year of her reign, Hatshepsut commissioned an inscription at a site called Wadi Maghara, 140 miles (225 km) west of Cairo, that shows her worshiping the god Soped and Thutmose III worshiping Hathor, who was the patron goddess of the turquoise industry.

This part of the red chapel is partially open to the elements, and includes a lustral, or sunken, basin, probably used for ceremonial purposes.

THE MISSION TO PUNT

In the eighth year of her regency, Hatshepsut commissioned an expedition to Punt in East Africa that was to prove one of the highlights of her reign. She was so proud of this mission that it was illustrated and described in great detail on the middle terrace walls of her memorial temple at Djeser Djeseru.

From the Old Kingdom onward, the Egyptians had sent trading missions to Punt. There is still some debate today as to the precise location and identity of this land. Research done on the plants and animals shown to have come from the region indicates that it was probably in what is now either southern Sudan or Eritrea. Punt was the source of many exotic products, including gold, African blackwood, ebony, ivory, and incense. There were also exotic animals like monkeys and baboons in the region, and there is also evidence that human slaves, including pygmies, were sold to the Egyptians. Pygmies often served as dancers or acrobats in temples.

Egyptian missions usually reached Punt by sailing north from Thebes to Coptos, then traveling overland from the Nile Valley to ports on the Red Sea coast, and from there sailing down the coast.

A VISUAL HISTORY

The mission is pictured in great detail at Djeser Djeseru. The scenes are set out like a story, with each stage given a separate scene. The images are colorful and lively, and the accuracy of the pictures, in particular the scenes in Africa, suggests that the artists who drew them on the temple walls had probably been on the mission and seen the sites for themselves. Hatshepsut describes how the trading mission was sent not by her, but by the god Amen. Above the first illustration, which shows boats setting sail southward, the inscription states, "Sailing in the sea . . . journeying in peace to the land of Punt . . . according to the command of the Lord of Gods, Amen Lord of Thebes . . . in order to bring for him the marvels of every country."

The next image shows the expedition landing at Punt. On the right of the scene Hatshepsut's vizier, Neshi, is shown at the head of a group of soldiers. A pile of goods is in front of him, including bracelets, necklaces, axes, and daggers. On the

Another relief in Hatshepsut's temple depicts members of her trading expedition to the Land of Punt.

left of the scene the Punt chieftain Perehu is shown at the head of a small group that includes his wife Eti, two sons and a daughter, and three male servants leading a donkey. Perehu is tall and thin with red skin and a pointed beard. His wife Eti is grotesquely fat with huge folds of flesh and enormous thighs visible through a see-through dress. Their village is also shown at the edge of a forest of ebony, palm, and incense trees. Their small, round houses set on stilts with pointed roofs are shown with ladders reaching up to their front doors.

The next scene shows the Egyptians having set up their own campsite. Neshi is standing in front of his tent inspecting produce brought by the Punt chieftain and his villagers. Neshi and Perehu have probably just had lunch together, as the inscription above reads: "There are offered to them bread, beer, wine, meat, fruit, everything found in Egypt." We don't know how long the Egyptians stayed in Punt, or whether they explored farther into the country with their new friends. However, in the next scene we are shown Puntites and Egyptians working together loading the ships with goods for the Egyptians' return journey. The inscription above the ships describes the cargo: "All goodly fragrant woods of God's land, heaps of myrrh resin, with fresh myrrh trees, with ebony and pure ivory, with green gold of emu, with cinnamon wood, khest wood, with ihmut incense, sonter incense, eye cosmetic, with apes, monkeys, dogs, and with skins of the southern panther, with natives and their children. Never was brought the like of this for any king who has been since the beginning."

The return trip back to Egypt is left to our imagination and the next scene shows Hatshepsut greeting the returning explorers at the banks of the Nile at Thebes. More goods are shown being unloaded onto the quay, including incense trees carried between two poles with their roots in baskets. Other men are carrying boomerangs, ebony, incense, and amphorae (large pottery jars) containing scented oils. There are men leading herds of cattle and an ape. The next scene shows Hatshepsut offering all the goods to Amen, and the inscription describes the action:

> The King himself, the King of Upper and Lower Egypt, Maatkare, presents the good things of Punt, the treasures of the divine land, together with the gifts of the countries of the south . . . to Amen, Lord of Thebes, presider over Karnak, for the sake of the life, prosperity, and health of the King of Upper and Lower Egypt, Maatkare, that she may live, abide, and her heart be joyful, that she may rule over the Two Lands like Ra forever.

This basalt statue of Thutmose III stands in the Temple of Amun at Karnak.

The final scenes show Hatshepsut announcing the success of her mission both to the god Amen and to her own courtiers. Thutmose III only appears once in the whole story, where he is shown offering "the best of fresh myrrh" to Amen. Neshi, Senenmut, and another unnamed official are shown congratulating Hatshepsut on the success of her mission.

THE QUEEN'S FINAL YEARS

As far as we can tell, the final years of Hatshepsut's reign passed peacefully. Ineni, the mayor of Thebes, and Hapuseneb, the chief priest of Amen, had died earlier in her reign. At some point between the sixteenth and twentieth years of her reign, her trusted servant Senenmut died. We have considerable evidence of her affection for this person. There are more than twenty-five statues of Senenmut throughout Egypt. Hatshepsut's memorial temple at Djeser Djeseru contains more than sixty small pictures of Senenmut hidden behind doors and statues. These statues and images would have ensured that Senenmut's ka continued after his death.

Senenmut had constructed for himself two magnificent tombs on the west bank of the Nile at Thebes, with one on top of the hill known as Gurna. This tomb was joined to that of the steward Amenhotep and another royal tutor called Senimen. Gurna also continued to be a popular location for government officials' tombs during the reign of Thutmose III. However, Senenmut wasn't satisfied with this location, and he also constructed a second tomb in the grounds of the Djeser Djeseru temple precinct. The entrance to this tomb was originally hidden in the floor of a large quarry. We do not know today where Senenmut was buried, as both tombs were found empty when excavated. Many of his monuments were defaced or destroyed at some point after his death, probably because of his close association with Hatshepsut.

Princess Neferure seems to have spent most of her adult years acting as official "wife" to her mother at various state functions. The role of queen (king's Great Wife) was often needed in religious and state ceremonies, and Hatshepsut sensibly used her daughter to fill in when necessary. The last mention of Neferure is in an inscription in Senenmut's Gurna tomb dated to the sixteenth year of Hatshepsut's reign, and Neferure seems to have died soon after. We do not know whether she was ever married to her half brother Thutmose III, and we also have no clear idea of how she felt about living out her life in the service of her mother.

From the twentieth year of her reign onward, Hatshepsut finally began to include Thutmose III as an equal partner in her monuments and inscriptions, where he was shown standing beside instead of behind her. She may have felt that she was getting old and would soon die and that it was important to ensure that the crown passed smoothly to her successor. Thutmose III was by now the commander in chief of Egypt's armies, and he was busy with a series of campaigns in Nubia, Syria, and Canaan. Hatshepsut died on the tenth day of the sixth month of her twenty-second year of rule (1458 BCE). For seventy days her body underwent ritual mummification and she was finally buried next to her father in her tomb (KV 20) in the Valley of the Kings.

Thutmose III went on to rule Egypt alone for more then thirty years. He was a great warrior and conducted seventeen military campaigns in Syria and many others in Nubia. He also constructed and enlarged many temples throughout Egypt and

THE SEARCH FOR HATSHEPSUT

In 1903, Howard Carter, the Egyptologist and archaeologist who had originally discovered the remains of the famous Egyptian emperor Tutankhamun, found two mummies. He discovered them in a small, undec-

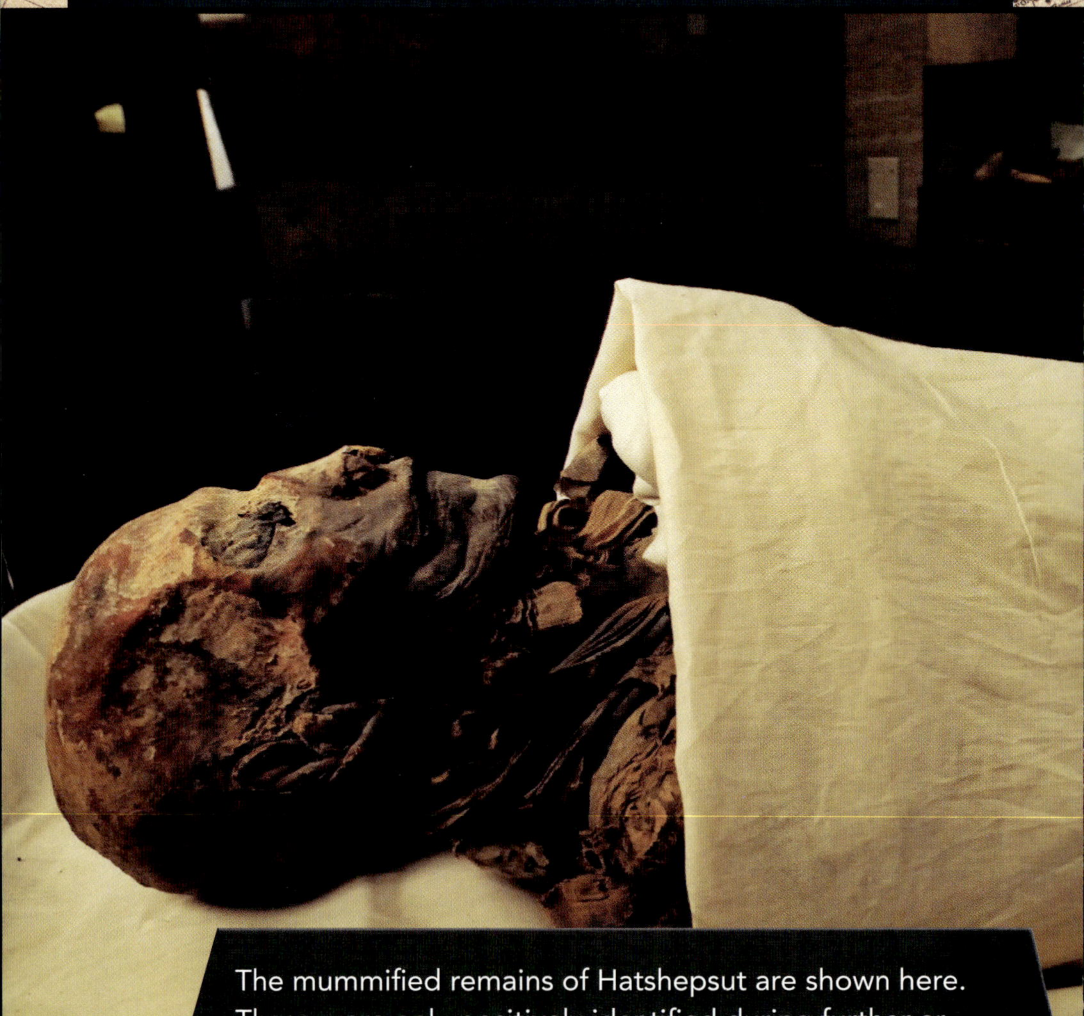

The mummified remains of Hatshepsut are shown here. These were only positively identified during further archaeological testing in 2007.

orated tomb, KV 60, in front of KV 20, the official tomb of Hatshepsut. They are among a series of secret tombs in the Valley of the Kings, some of which housed a number of high-ranking Egyptians who remained unidentified.

One of the discovered mummies was that of a small woman in a coffin inscribed with markings confirming she was a royal nurse. This was believed to be Hatshepsut's wet nurse, Sitre. The other was another woman, discovered on the floor next to the nurse's coffin. Some believed this could indeed be Hatshepsut herself.

In 2007, Dr. Zahi Hawass, the official chief archaeologist, undertook the work necessary to clear up this mystery. There were many doubts that the other woman indeed was Hatshepsut. The woman was thought to be too large. But new forensic tools—including an X-ray computed tomography (CT) scan and dental matching techniques—confirmed that it was indeed the long-lost female pharaoh.

This face of Hatshepsut comes from a colossal statue made of painted limestone that stood at the pharaoh's Mortuary Temple.

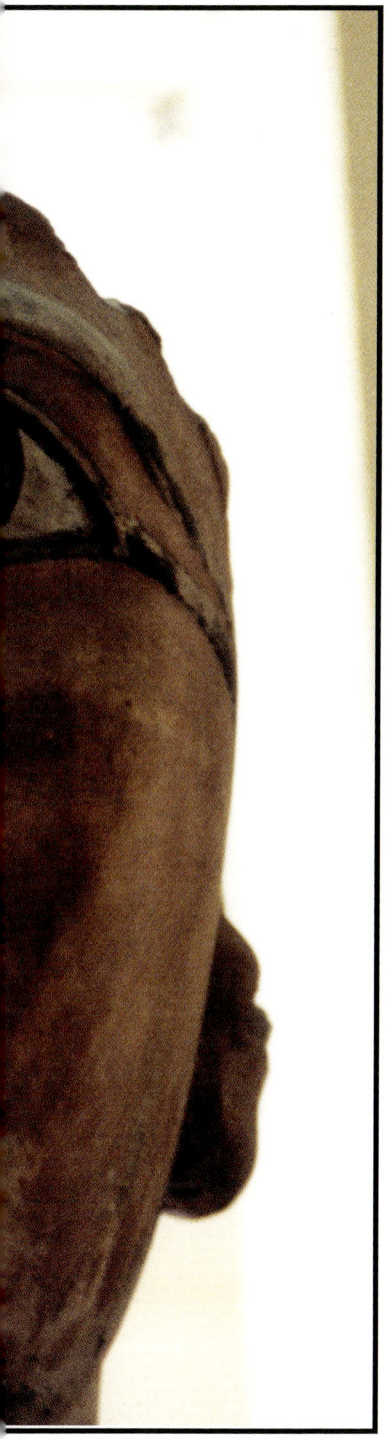

Nubia. Thutmose III is remembered as one of Egypt's greatest pharaohs. He died in 1425 BCE and his mummy is now in the Cairo Museum. Toward the end of his reign, Thutmose began the systematic destruction of the statues, images, and written inscriptions of his aunt and stepmother, Hatshepsut. However, he attacked only those representations that showed her as king. He left alone those showing Hatshepsut as royal daughter, royal wife, and royal mother. This was probably because he finally decided that the existence of a pharaoh who was a woman was against Maat and that Hatshepsut's existence as Egypt's female pharaoh set a dangerous example for other royal women.

cultivation The season between September and April during which crops were planted and ripened.

dynasty A series of rulers of a country linked by bloodline.

God's Wife of Amen An important temple post at Karnak, usually filled by the wife or mother of the pharaoh.

harvest The season between April and June when crops were gathered.

Heb-Sed Festival The ritual of royal regeneration, usually celebrated after thirty years of the king's reign.

inundation The term used to describe both the event and the season of the annual flooding of the Nile, which took place between June and September.

ka In the Egyptian religion, the life force of every person. A person's ka was born at the same time as him or her, and existed throughout his or her life. When an individual died, the ka continued to live on

kemet The name for Egypt used in ancient times, meaning "Black Land." It refers to the fertile Nile mud that washed over the land when the Nile flooded.

king lists A group of sources listing the names and titles of past kings in succession. Most lists have been found in tombs or temples.

Lower Egypt The northern half of the country

stretching from Memphis to the Mediterranean coast.

Maat Denotes both a goddess who embodied aspects of truth, justice, and the concept of harmony in the universe.

memorial temple A temple where the mortuary cult of the king was celebrated.

Memphis The capital city of ancient Egypt, near Cairo.

Nubia The region immediately south of ancient Egypt, approximating modern Sudan.

pharaoh From the New Kingdom onward, the term most commonly used for the Egyptian king.

Upper Egypt The southern half of the country stretching from Memphis to Aswan.

Valley of the Kings A New Kingdom royal necropolis located on the west bank of the Nile, about three miles west of modern Luxor.

vizier The chief minister of the government. During the New Kingdom there were two viziers, one at Memphis and another at Thebes.

FOR MORE INFORMATION

American Research Center in Egypt (U.S. Office)
8700 Crownhill Boulevard, Suite 507
San Antonio, Texas 78209-1130
Email: info@arce.org
(210) 821.7000
Website: http://www.arce.org
The American Research Center in Egypt (ARCE), via its presence in Egypt and in cities around the world, supports extensive scholarship, training, and conservation efforts in Egypt.

Ancient Egypt Alive
http://www.ancientegyptalive.com
Ancient Egypt Alive is a Canadian organization devoted to raising interest, knowledge, and excitement around the study and preservation of ancient Egyptian history and culture.

Ancient Egypt Research Association (AERA)
26 Lincoln Street, Suite 5
Brighton, MA 02135
(617) 783-0737
Website: http://www.aeraweb.org
Ancient Egypt Research Association's mission is to advance archaeological research, conservation, and training in Egypt, with a focus on ancient settlement and the archaeology of the Giza Pyramids Plateau.

International Association of Egyptologists (USA Branch)
Department of Ancient Egyptian, Nubian, and Far Eastern Art
Museum of Fine Arts
465 Huntington Avenue
Boston, MA 02115
Website: http://www.iae-egyptology.org
The International Association of Egyptologists is a professional association for scholars, historians, archaeologists, and others working all over the world to promote Egyptology.

The National Geographic Society
145 17th Street NW
Washington, DC 20036
(202) 862-8638
Website: http://www.nationalgeographic.com
The National Geographic Society, famous for its publication, National Geographic magazine, is a global nonprofit organization committed to exploring the world and protecting its natural and historical resources and sites.

WEBSITES

Because of the changing number of internet links, Rosen Publishing has developed an online list of websites related to the subject of this book. This site is updated regularly. Please use this link to access this list:

http://www.rosenlinks.com/LANW/hatsh

FOR FURTHER READING

Cooney, Kara. *The Woman Who Would Be King: Hatshepsut's Rise to Power in Ancient Egypt*. New York, NY: Crown, 2014.

Bierbrier, Morris. *The Tomb-Builders of the Pharaohs*. Cairo, Egypt: American University in Cairo Press, 2016.

Brier, Bob. *Cleopatra's Needles: The Lost Obelisks of Egypt*. New York, NY: Bloomsbury, 2016.

Eaton-Krauss, Marianne. *The Unknown Tutankhamun*. New York, NY: Bloomsbury, 2015.

Fletcher, Joann. *The Story of Egypt: The Civilization that Shaped the World*. New York, NY: Pegasus Books, 2016.

Hagen, Rose-Marie, and Rainer Hagen. *Egypt: People, Gods, Pharaohs*. New York, NY: Taschen, 2016.

Hayes, William. *The Scepter of Egypt 2: The Hyksos Period and the New Kingdom*. New York, NY: Metropolitan Museum of Art, 1990.

Reeves, Nicholas, and Richard Wilkinson. *The Complete Valley of the Kings*. London, United Kingdom: Thames and Hudson, 1996.

Robins, Gay. *Women in Ancient Egypt*. London, United Kingdom : British Museum Press, 1993.

Roller, Duane W. *Cleopatra: A Biography*. New York, NY: Oxford University Press, 2011.

Shaw, Ian, and Paul Nicholson. *British Museum Dictionary of Ancient Egypt*. London, United Kingdom: British Museum Press, 1995.

Stevenson Smith, William. *The Art and Architecture of Ancient Egypt*. New Haven, CT: Yale University Press, 1998.

Tyldesley, Joyce. *Cleopatra: Last Queen of Egypt*. New York, NY: Basic Books, 2008.

Wilkinson, Toby. *The Rise and Fall of Ancient Egypt*. New York, NY: Random House, 2011.

Aldred, Cyril. *The Egyptians*. London, United Kingdom: Thames & Hudson, 1998.

Baines, John, and Jaromir Malek. *Atlas of Ancient Egypt*. New York, NY: Facts on File, 1993.

Breasted, James. *Ancient Records of Egypt*. Vol. 2: *The Eighteenth Dynasty*. Chicago, IL: University of Chicago Press, 2001.

Davies, Vivian, and Renee Friedman. *Egypt Uncovered*. New York, NY: Stewart, Tabori & Chang, 1998.

Hayes, William. *The Scepter of Egypt 2: The Hyksos Period and the New Kingdom*. New York, NY: Metropolitan Museum of Art, 1990.

Lichtheim, Miriam. *Ancient Egyptian Literature*. Vol. 2: *The New Kingdom*. Berkeley, CA: University of California Press, 1976.

Naville, Edouard. *The Temple of Deir el-Bahari*. London, United Kingdom: Egypt Exploration Fund, 1895–1908.

Reeves, Nicholas, and Richard Wilkinson. *The Complete Valley of the Kings*. London, United Kingdom: Thames and Hudson, 1996.

Robins, Gay. *Women in Ancient Egypt*. London, United Kingdom: British Museum Press, 1993.

Shaw, Ian, and Paul Nicholson. *British Museum Dictionary of Ancient Egypt*. London, United Kingdom: British Museum Press, 1995.

Snape, Steven. *Egyptian Temples*. Princes Risborough, England: Shire, 1996.

Stevenson Smith, William. *The Art and Architecture of Ancient Egypt*. New Haven, CT: Yale University Press, 1998.

Tyldesley, Joyce. *Hatshepsut the Female Pharaoh*. London, United Kingdom: Viking, 1996.

Waterson, Barbara. *Women in Ancient Egypt*. New York: St Martin's Press, 1991.

ABOUT THE AUTHORS

Margaux Baum is a writer and editor from Queens, New York.

Susanna Thomas has a BA in Egyptian archaeology from University College, London, and was awarded a PhD from Liverpool University in 2000. She has worked at sites all over Egypt, including in the Valley of the Kings, and runs excavations at Tell Abqa'in in the western delta. She is particularly interested in vitreous materials and trade in the late Bronze Age. She is currently a research fellow at Liverpool University and director of the Ramesside Fortress Town Project.

PHOTO CREDITS

Cover, p. 3 De Agostini/C. Sappa/Getty Images; cover (background), pp. 58–59 Héctor de Pereda Photography/Moment/Getty Images; pp. 7, 91 Universal Images Group/Getty Images; pp. 12–13 Bruce Yuanyue Bi/Lonely Planet Images/Getty Images; pp. 15, 100–101 De Agostini/W. Buss/Getty Images; pp. 18–19 Universal History Archive/UIG/Bridgeman Images; pp. 24–25, 82–83 Jaroslav Havlicek/EyeEm/Getty Images; pp. 28–29, 46 Print Collector/Hulton Archive/Getty Images; p. 34 DEA/G. Sioen/De Agostini Picture Library/Getty Images; pp. 38–39 Valley of the Nobles, Thebes, Egypt/Bridgeman Images; p. 43 Museum of Fine Arts, Boston, Massachusetts, USA/Gift of Theodore M. Davis/Bridgeman Images; pp. 44–45, 84–85 De Agostini Picture Library/Getty Images; p. 50 Universal History Archive/Universal Images Group/Getty Images; p. 53, 80 De Agostini/G. Dagli Orti/Getty Images; pp. 62–63 Richard Nowitz/National Geographic Image Collection/Getty Images; p. 67 © Eye Ubiquitous/Alamy Stock Photo; pp. 72–73 © Mike P Shepherd/Alamy; pp. 76–77 DEA/G. Dagli Orti/De Agostini/Getty Images; p. 88 Werner Forman/Universal Images Group/Getty Images; p. 94 DEA/S. Vannini/De Agostini/Getty Images; pp. 98–99 Cris Bouroncle/AFP/Getty Images; interior pages background images © iStockphoto.com/kikkalek5050 (sky), Triff/Shutterstock.com (map)

Designer: Brian Garvey; Editor: Philip Wolny; Photo Researcher: Philip Wolny